SUPERSTITIONS SURROUNDING
FRIDAY THE 13TH

Tammy Gagne

Stride
An Imprint of The Child's World®
childsworld.com

Published by The Child's World®
800-599-READ • childsworld.com

Copyright © 2023 by The Child's World®
All rights reserved. No part of this book may be reproduced or utilized in any form or by any means without written permission from the publisher.

Photography Credits
Photographs ©: Shutterstock Images, cover, 1, 4, 9, 15, 19; iStockphoto, 5; Renata Sedmakova/Shutterstock Images, 7; Árni Magnússon Institute/Wikimedia, 8; Everett Collection/Shutterstock Images, 11, 16, 18; Sol Stock/iStockphoto, 12; AP Images, 14; Alvaro Atalaya/Shutterstock Images, 20

ISBN Information
9781503865105 (Reinforced Library Binding)
9781503866430 (Portable Document Format)
9781503867277 (Online Multi-user eBook)
9781503868113 (Electronic Publication)

LCCN 2022939518

Printed in the United States of America

About the Author
Tammy Gagne has written hundreds of books for both adults and children. Some of her recent books have been about desert ecosystems and space tourism. She lives in northern New England with her husband, son, and dogs.

CONTENTS

CHAPTER ONE
A Day Linked to Bad Luck . . . 4

CHAPTER TWO
From the Imagination of a Writer . . . 10

CHAPTER THREE
Believers and Nonbelievers . . . 14

Glossary . . . 22
Fast Facts . . . 23
One Stride Further . . . 23
Find Out More . . . 24
Index . . . 24

CHAPTER ONE

A DAY LINKED TO BAD LUCK

The belief that certain dates can bring good or bad luck has been around for thousands of years. Science does not support this **superstition**. But many people still believe it is true. One of the most popular superstitions is that Friday the 13th is an unlucky date. Some people even change their plans on this day from fear of bad luck.

Friday the 13th can happen up to three times in one calendar year.

There are people who study the Christian Bible. Some of them believe that a couple of bad events described in the Bible happened on Fridays. For example, some people think Adam and Eve disobeyed God on a Friday. In the Bible, God created Adam and Eve. Some people believe that they were the first humans on Earth. God told Adam and Eve not to eat from the Tree of Knowledge. But they did anyway. This led God to force Adam and Eve to leave a paradise called the Garden of Eden.

Other significant events in the Bible may have happened on Fridays, too. It is said that Cain murdered his brother Abel on a Friday. And some say Noah was forced to launch his gigantic ark on this day of the week due to an enormous flood.

Good Friday is a Christian holiday remembering Jesus's death. Babies born on Good Friday are said to be lucky.

The Bible also tells a story about a 13th dinner guest who brings **misfortune**. Judas was the 13th guest at the Last Supper. This was the last meal Jesus shared with his followers. Judas betrayed Jesus, who was put to death the next day, a Friday.

Friday the 13th is not the only date believed to bring bad luck. In Greece, Tuesday the 13th is said to be bad luck. A superstition in Italy states that Friday the 17th is unlucky.

Loki is a Norse god who is best known for his tricks and ability to change shape.

In Norway, **mythology** links the number 13 to Loki. He is the Norse god of mischief. In one myth, Loki was the 13th god to arrive at a **banquet**. Hodr and Balder were also there. Hodr was the god of night and darkness. Balder was the god of joy and goodness. They were brothers. But Loki tricked Hodr into killing Balder at the event. Once again, the number 13 appears linked to misfortune.

CHAPTER TWO

FROM THE IMAGINATION OF A WRITER

Until 1907, Fridays and the number 13 were seen as unlucky, but they were not connected to each other. Then Thomas Larson wrote a book that paired the two unlucky things. *Friday, the Thirteenth* was the book's title. The main character planned to crash the **stock market** on that date. When the stock market crashes, people lose money they have invested in it. At the time the book came out, the date was still not known for being unlucky.

Some stock market traders in the United States used to wear hats on Friday the 13th to protect themselves from evil spirits.

According to some people, wearing red on Friday the 13th is one way to avoid bad luck.

But a year later, a popular newspaper reminded the public of the story. An article in the *New York Times* referred to the date as one to fear. Superstitious people started to believe that bad things were more likely to happen on Friday the 13th. Over time, more people heard about the superstition and believed it.

Some people adjust their habits when the 13th falls on a Friday. They avoid doing anything too risky. There is nothing really unlucky about the date. But the superstition affects the world in real ways. For example, airlines sell fewer tickets on Friday the 13th. Travelers who are willing to fly on that day get cheaper seats for this reason.

A series of popular horror movies is based on the Friday the 13th superstition. By 2022, there were 12 movies in the series. The main character was born on Friday the 13th and brings others bad luck on this date.

CHAPTER THREE

BELIEVERS AND NONBELIEVERS

Some well-known people believed that Friday the 13th is unlucky. U.S. president Franklin D. Roosevelt would not plan to start any trips on that date. Ford Motor Company founder Henry Ford would not do any business on Friday the 13th for fear of bad luck.

The Ford Motor Company started making cars in the early 1900s.

The fear of the number 13 is called triskaidekaphobia.

U.S. president Theodore Roosevelt was a member of a 13 club. The group got together every month on the 13th to celebrate the number 13.

In addition, both President Roosevelt and President Herbert Hoover avoided having dinner parties with 13 guests. A related superstition states that it is unlucky for 13 people to be in the same room. But not everyone takes the fear of this number so seriously. Some people go out of their way to gather in groups of 13. Many so-called 13 clubs have been formed for this purpose. Members gather in this number just to go against the superstition. Some other U.S. presidents have been members. Chester A. Arthur and Theodore Roosevelt are two of them.

Some people think that 13 is a lucky number. Taylor Swift is one of them. The pop singer was born on December 13th and turned 13 on Friday the 13th. She has said in interviews that many good things in her career have been tied to the number 13, too.

Taylor Swift rose to fame in the mid-2000s.

In Judaism, the number 13 has been considered a sign of strength and luck. There are 13 principles of Jewish faith, and boys are considered men when they turn 13.

Some people dread Friday the 13th. Others just see it as an ordinary day.

Like other superstitions, the one about Friday the 13th bringing bad luck is not based in scientific fact. There is no proof that the date brings good or bad luck. But a lot of people still believe in this superstition.

The number 13 is so feared in some places that it is skipped over. In some skyscrapers and hospitals, the floor directly above the 12th floor is called the 14th floor. Many airports also skip the number 13 for their gates.

GLOSSARY

banquet (BANG-kwit) A banquet is a large dinner held in someone's honor. Loki was the 13th guest at a banquet in a Norse myth.

misfortune (mis-FOR-chuhn) Misfortune refers to events that have distressing or unfortunate results. Some people believe that Friday the 13th brings misfortune.

mythology (mih-THOL-uh-jee) Mythology is a group of stories about the gods and heroes of a particular culture. Loki was the god of mischief in Norse mythology.

stock market (STOK MAR-kit) The stock market is a place where people buy and sell shares in companies. A book about the stock market inspired the superstition about Friday the 13th.

superstition (soo-pur-STIH-shuhn) A superstition is a belief that certain events cause good or bad luck. The belief that Friday the 13th is an unlucky day is a superstition.

FAST FACTS

- Some people believe the superstition about Friday the 13th being an unlucky day.

- The Bible and Norse mythology include stories where a 13th guest at a gathering brought bad luck.

- Some people avoid doing certain activities on Friday the 13th due to fear of the superstition.

- There is no scientific evidence that Friday the 13th brings bad luck.

ONE STRIDE FURTHER

- Have you ever experienced bad luck on Friday the 13th? If so, do you think it was a coincidence, or do you believe in the superstition?

- How might a person gather scientific evidence that Friday the 13th either does or does not cause bad luck?

- Why do you think people believe in this superstition?

FIND OUT MORE

IN THE LIBRARY

Alexander, Heather. *A Child's Introduction to Norse Mythology.* New York, NY: Black Dog & Leventhal Publishers, 2018.

Gagne, Tammy. *Lucky Numbers.* Parker, CO: The Child's World, 2023.

Johnson, C. M. *Superstitions.* Minneapolis, MN: Lerner, 2018.

ON THE WEB

Visit our website for links about Friday the 13th:

childsworld.com/links

Note to Parents, Teachers, and Librarians: We routinely verify our Web links to make sure they are safe and active sites. So encourage your readers to check them out!

INDEX

airlines, 13

banquet, 9
Bible, 6–7

Garden of Eden, 6
Greece, 7

hospitals, 21

Italy, 7

misfortune, 7, 9
mythology, 9

Norway, 9

president, 14, 17

stock market, 10

24